ショーン・マイケル・ウィルソン 原作
Makiko Kodama 画

深井 裕美子 訳

JN189806

講談社
Kodansha Bilingual Comics

まえがき

　講談社から3冊目のバイリンガル・コミックスを出すことになりました。作画はMakiko Kodamaです。長編デビューとなる本作で、Makikoは、どことなくヨーロッパの香りのする、すてきな絵を描いてくれました。

　この作品のストーリーはシンプルです。日本にやってきたデイヴィッドとマリーという外国人。五輪開幕が間近に迫る東京を、二人の友人タケシが案内します。2020年大会の会場や競技を紹介する架空の本が登場するほか、1964年大会以降の東京の変化や日本人初参加の1912年大会、そして行方不明のランナー、金栗四三に関する有名な逸話などが取り上げられています。五輪前、五輪開催中、そして五輪後に東京を訪れる外国人のガイドブックにもなる本です。

　日本の読者のために、よく使う英会話のフレーズも随所に散りばめられています。外国の友人や訪問客に出会ったら、ぜひ使ってみてください。あなたのためにもなりますし、日本の国際化の一助にもなります。

　どうぞ、この本を存分にお楽しみください。

　　　　　　ショーン・マイケル・ウィルソン

Preface

This is my third bilingual comic book with Kodansha and the first full length book by Makiko Kodama. She has done a good job with some lovely artwork in a style that has a slightly European feel.

The story is a simple one: two foreigners, David and Marie, visit Japan. Their Japanese friend, Takeshi, guides them around Tokyo as the city prepares for the Games to start. We see pages from a fictitious guidebook they have that gives basic information about the Olympics, such as the various venues and the games that will be played in 2020. In addition to this, it mentions the way Tokyo has changed since the 1964 Olympics, and also about the 1912 Games when Japan first participated, together with the famous story of the runner who went missing, Shiso Kanakuri. So this manga can be used as a guidebook for visitors to Tokyo before or during the Olympics and after that as well.

Our book also has various pages on English conversation tips that can help Japanese readers understand common phrases. Please don't be shy to use such English with foreign friends or visitors—it's good for you and for helping Japan become more international.

I hope you enjoy our new book!

Sean Michael Wilson

Contents
もくじ

Preface   p.   2
まえがき

Part 1: Welcome to Japan!   p.   5
ようこそ日本へ！
Conversation Tips #1   p. 36
会話のコツ①

Part 2: Tokyo, the Changing City   p. 37
変化し続ける街、東京
Conversation Tips #2   p. 70
会話のコツ②

Part 3: Guide to the 2020 Olympics   p. 71
2020オリンピックガイド
Conversation Tips #3   p. 98
会話のコツ③

Part 4: Epilogue—Opening Ceremony   p. 99
エピローグ〜開会式
Conversation Tips #4   p.109
会話のコツ④

Part 1: Welcome to Japan!
ようこそ日本へ！

歴史ある会場
Built for the 1964 Tokyo Olympics
1964年東京オリンピックのために建設

Yoyogi National Stadium
国立代々木競技場

Nippon Budokan
日本武道館

成田空港

Narita Airport

ロンドン(ヒースロー)

006

① Remove all clothing (including underwear and bathing wear) before you go into the bathroom or the bathtub.

① 洗い場ならびに湯船に入る前に、すべての衣服(下着・水着を含む)を脱いでください。

② Rinse your body, using a shower or water scooped from the tub, before you go into the bathtub.

② 湯船に入る前に、シャワーまたは湯船から汲んだお湯で体を洗ってください。

③ No towels, washcloths, shampoo or soap in the bathtub, please.

③ 湯船にはタオル、ボディタオル、シャンプー、石鹸は入れないでください。

④ No bathing while, or after, drinking alcohol.

④ 入浴中または直前の飲酒はしないでください。

⑤ Wipe yourself dry, using a towel or similar item, before returning to the dressing room.

⑤ 脱衣室に戻る前に、タオルなどを使って体の雫を拭ってください。

026

OK, I have to wash myself first.

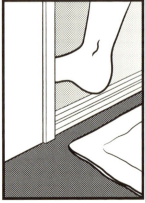

まず体を洗うのね。

そうね。今ものすごく眠いの。
気持ちいいお風呂と食事のせいだと思う。　　　　今日は早めに休む？

明日なんだけど、10時頃にホテルに来てくれるんだっけ？

うん。一緒にガイドブックを見て、行く先を決めよう。いい？

もちろん。ありがとう、タケシ。メルシー。

また明日！

こちらこそ。
じゃあまた明日！

上手なおじぎだ！

会話のコツ①

日常会話で便利に使える言い回しをピックアップしました。ここでは紹介や道案内で言うフレーズを見てみましょう。

☐ **This is <u>my girlfriend Marie</u>.** ガールフレンドのマリーだ。(p.9)
　人を紹介するときはこのように切り出すことができます。下線部には相手のことを表わす言葉を入れましょう。また、名前を先に出す言い方もあります。
例) This is <u>my coworker James</u>. 同僚のジェイムズです。
　　This is <u>Anna, my daughter</u>. 娘のアンナです。

☐ **Can I help you?** 手伝おうか？(p.10)
　手を差し伸べるときに言う万能のフレーズ。ていねいに言いたいときはMayを使います。
例) May I help you? 手伝いましょうか？

☐ **This way to <u>the trains</u>.** 電車の乗り場はこっちだよ。(p.11)
　ある場所へ案内するとき、便利に使えるフレーズです。会話では文頭にIt'sが付いたり付かなかったりします。下線部に入れる単語を変えて応用しましょう。
例) This way to <u>the stadium</u>. スタジアムはこっちだよ。
　　It's this way to <u>Shibuya Station</u>. 渋谷駅はこっちです。

☐ **There you go.** はい、どうぞ。(p.21)
　相手に何かを差し出すときに使いましょう。Hereを使ったバリエーションもあります。
例) Here you go. はい、どうぞ。

☐ **Sorry to keep you waiting.** お待たせしました。(p.25)
　待ち合わせに遅れたときのほか、電話口で相手を待たせたときにも使えます。待たされたことを気にしていない場合は、次のように答えましょう。
例) No problem. いいえ／平気だよ。
　　I'm fine. 大丈夫だよ。

☐ **Are you ready to eat?** お腹空いてる？(p.31)
　このほかに、次のようにも言えます。
例) Are you hungry? お腹空いてる？
　　Do you want to have something to eat? 何か食べる？

Part 2:
Tokyo, the Changing City
変化し続ける街、東京

Games with History

歴史の長い競技

The first modern Olympics were held in 1896;
the first Paralympic Games, in1960.
近代オリンピックの第1回大会は1896年、
初のパラリンピック大会は1960年に実施。

Archery (Paralympics)
—since Rome 1960
アーチェリー(パラリンピック)
—1960年ローマ大会より

Marathon (Olympics)
—since Athens 1896
マラソン(オリンピック)
—1896年アテネ大会より

どうやったらお湯が出るんだろう。

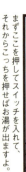

How does the hot water come out of this?

It's not working?

I'm pressing the buttons but nothing is happening.

Ah, you need to press this one to turn it on and then this one for the hot water to come out.

まずここを押してスイッチを入れて、それからこっちを押せばお湯が出ますよ。

うまくいかない？

ボタンを押してるんだけど何も出ないんだ。

It can be a bit confusing if there is no English explanation.

Oh, thanks. We just arrived in Japan yesterday and don't know how things work yet.

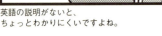

英語の説明がないと、ちょっとわかりにくいですよね。

ありがとうございます。昨日日本に着いたばかりで、まだよくわからなくて。

それはいい
アイディアだね。 そのガイドブックの写真を見ながら東京見物をすると、
1960年代からどれほど変わったかわかるよ。

あ、古いものがあったわ。

この辺りだけ見ても、ほとんどのものが新しくて、古い建物は見当たらないね。

これこそ僕が思ってた
日本のイメージだ。

回復するのに
5日もかかった。

船とシベリア鉄道を乗り継いで18日間の旅だった。
スウェーデンに着いた頃には金栗はふらふらで、

. . . and needed 5 days to recover.

Tired...

Unfortunately,

It took 18 days to get there by ship and the Trans-Siberian railway. Kanakuri was exhausted when they arrived in Sweden . . .

あいにく金栗のマラソン足袋（現在も工事現場で用いられる、指先が割れたキャンバス地の履物）も功を奏する事はなかった。

マラソン競技の日、スウェーデンは猛暑で、多くの選手が脱水症状で倒れてしまった。

Kanakuri was not helped by the tabi shoes he wore—two-toed canvas shoes still worn today by construction workers.

there was a heat wave in Sweden during the marathon and many of the runners collapsed from hyperthermia.

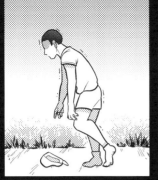

FLUMMPP

体調不良と成績不振を恥じた金栗は、スウェーデンを去った。しかしそのことが大会運営事務局に伝えられなかったため、金栗の記録は「行方不明」とされた。

In shame at his sickness and poor performance, Kanakuri left Sweden. But the Swedish authorities were not informed, so they listed him as MISSING.

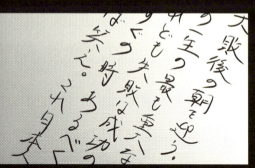

I will regret my performance for as long as I live. Yet, this failure could inspire future success.

行方不明の日本人ランナー

Missing Japanese Runner!

Amazingly, he was listed as "missing" by Sweden for more than 50 years!

驚くことに、金栗は50年以上にわたってスウェーデンの名簿に「行方不明」と掲載され続けた。

But in 1967 a Swedish television broadcaster contacted him, suggesting that he finish the marathon—even though he was now 74 years old!

しかし1967年になって、スウェーデンの放送局が連絡をしてきた。74歳になっていた金栗に、ゴールしないかというのである。

He accepted the challenge.

金栗は申し出を受けた。

Oh, that reminds me! I read an article that said there was a lot of damage to Japan's environment because of the construction for the 1964 Olympics.

Oh, really? I've never heard that.

Hold on. It was in October? So why are the 2020 ones held in July when it's so hot?

Yes, I heard some people say that! I don't know why.

Yeah, it said that the high speed Shinkansen didn't need to be built between Tokyo and Osaka because no games took place in Osaka then.

And an expressway was built over some famous old bridge, spoiling the view and making the river under more polluted.

何ヵ月か前にメールで教えてくれたじゃないか。

なんで知ってるの?

You told me about it a few months ago, online. Remember?

Yes. How did you know about that?

This is the key man involved in the 1964 Tokyo Games— Masaji Tabata.

この人は当時のキーマンだった田畑政治という人だよ。

NHKの大河ドラマでも主役の一人だったよね?

そうか。忘れてた。

Oh, yes. I forgot. Ha ha . . .

He co-starred in the NHK *taiga* drama, right?

田畑は日本水泳連盟会長で、監督でもあった。機知に富み、長年根気強く活動した田畑は、日本初の五輪開催を成功に導いた。

Tabata was the president and coach of the Japan Swimming Federation. His resourcefulness and perseverance over decades led to Japan hosting the Olympics for the first time.

たとえば1948年のこと。日本とドイツがロンドン五輪への参加を認められなかったため、田畑は同じ時期に日本選手権水泳競技大会を開催した。大いに刺激を受けた古橋廣之進らは、ロンドン五輪で金メダルを獲得した選手よりも好タイムを出した。

For example, as Japan and Germany were excluded from the 1948 London Olympics, he scheduled the Japan National Swimming Championships to be held at the same time. Some swimmers then, like Furuhashi Hironoshin, were so inspired that they recorded better times than those that earned gold medals in the London Games!

1964年の五輪では大勢の外国人が日本を訪れた。近代日本のイメージは、このときにできあがったのではないかな。

Of course, a lot of foreign visitors came in 1964 and I think much of the modern image of Japan comes from this time.

They were impressed by the excellent preparations and how smoothly things went. This was, in a way, Japan coming into the modern post-war world.

彼らは日本人の綿密な事前準備とスムーズな進行に感心した。いわば、戦後の現代社会に日本がデビューした瞬間だったんだ。

明治時代に陸軍関係者のための娯楽施設が作られたのを皮切りに、1945年以降は米軍向けのバーやクラブ、60年代から70年代にはディスコがたくさんできた。長い時間をかけて、閉鎖的なお堅い場所から、誰もが来られるナイトライフの町に変わってきたんだ。

First, leisure places opened up for the Japanese troops in the Meiji era, then bars and clubs for the US troops after 1945, then discos in the 60s and 70s. So, throughout history, it changed from being a very private serious place to a very open nightlife place!

すごい変化だね。

Still, I'm quite keen to see what it's like.

OK, maybe we can go out for a drink later.

Oh, that's no good. They should have a wider variety.

It's a big change!

Yes. Actually, I don't like the nightlife there.

And the music they play now is terrible! It's 90 percent J-pop, K-pop, and mainstream hip-hop.

あなた、僕に夜のディスコに好きじゃないんだ。

わかったよ。
じゃあ、あとで飲みに行こう。

でも、どんな感じか見てみたいな。

それはだめね。
もっといろいろないと。

かかる音楽も嫌い。9割方J-POPとK-POP、そしてメインストリームのヒップホップだから。

063

会話のコツ②

簡単な単語の組み合わせでこんな意味になるんだ！という表現を中心に見てみます。

☐ **In some ways, yes.** 一部はね。(p.40)
　質問に対して部分的に肯定するときにこう言い、また、「そうとも言えるね」の意味にもなります。「でも…」と続けて、会話を発展させてみましょう。
例)Are you good at sports? スポーツは得意？
　—In some ways, yes. I like ball games, but I'm bad at swimming. 一部はね。球技は好きだけど、泳ぎはダメ。

☐ **First off** on our Tokyo Tour we have Shibuya Station.
　東京観光の最初は、渋谷駅だ。(p.42)
　first off … は「最初に、まず」という意味で、口語ではよく使われます。
例)OK, first off let's have lunch at that Indian restaurant. まずはあのインド料理店でお昼を食べよう。
　First off I'd like to introduce you to Jasmine, who coordinated this event. 最初に、このイベントの調整をしてくれたジャスミンをご紹介します。

☐ It's just so **moving** to be standing in exactly the same place as my grandmother.
　感動しちゃったんだ。おばあさんと同じ場所に来たと思ったら。(p.47)
　「感動した」はmovingで表せます。いろいろな場面で応用が利く表現です。
例)His speech was moving. 彼のスピーチには感動した。
　The rugby sevens match between Japan and Ireland was so moving!
　7人制ラグビーの日本対アイルランド戦はすごく感動的だった！

☐ **Hold on.** ちょっと待って。(p.58)
　相手に待ってほしいときや、違う意見を言う前によく使うフレーズです。
例)Hold on, I can't find my ticket. ちょっと待って、チケットが見つからない。
　Hold on. I thought we were going to Yokohama Stadium, not Tokyo Dome.
　ちょっと待って。東京ドームじゃなくて、横浜スタジアムに行くんだと思ってた。

☐ **What else would you like to do <u>today</u>?** 今日は他に何がしたい？(p.65)
　観光に連れて行っている相手にこう聞けば、具体的な答えがかえってくるでしょう。下線部はtomorrow「明日」やnext Saturday「今度の土曜」などに変えられます。
例)What else would you like to do <u>on Sunday</u>, Kim? キムは日曜日に他に何がしたい？
　—Well, I'd like to visit Nikko. 日光に行ってみたいなあ。

070

Part 3:
Guide to the 2020 Olympics
2020オリンピックガイド

新しい競技
Debuting at the Tokyo 2020 Games
2020年東京大会より実施

Badminton (Paralympics)
バドミントン(パラリンピック)

Sport Climbing (Olympics)
スポーツクライミング(オリンピック)

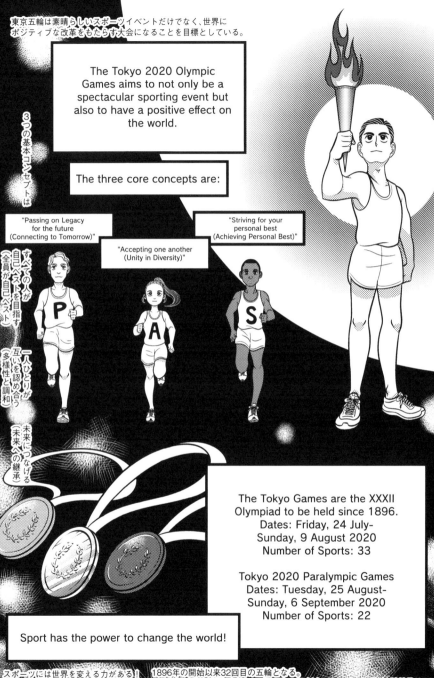

東京2020大会の会場計画は、
1964年の東京大会のレガシーを引き継ぐ「ヘリテッジゾーン」、
都市の未来を象徴する「東京ベイゾーン」の2つのゾーンから構成されています。

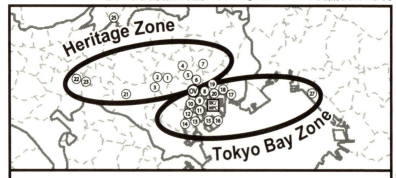

There are two areas where the games will take place—the "Heritage Zone" which houses several iconic venues used at the Tokyo 1964 Games and further sustains the enduring legacy of Tokyo 1964; and the "Tokyo BayZone" which serves as a model for innovative urban development and symbolises the exciting future of the city. *

選手村を中心に広がる2つのゾーンは、無限大の記号をイメージさせます。

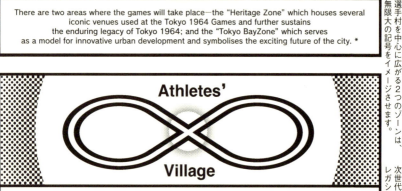

These two zones expand across the city to form an 'infinity' symbol with the Athletes' Village positioned at the point where the two zones intersect—at the physical and spiritual heart of the Games.*

無限大の記号は、トップアスリートが灯した情熱と、次世代へつながる可能性、そして語りつがれるレガシーが無限に広がっていくことを表しています。

無限の興奮？何日間かの興奮で十分だよ。僕には無理かも。

"Infinite excitement"? I don't think I could handle that. A few days of excitement will do just fine, thanks.

Ha ha!

わはは。

The 'infinity' symbol embodies the boundless passion, commitment and inspiration of the world's elite athletes, the limitless potential of future generations, and the lasting legacy that will be passed on to the people of Tokyo, Japan and the world.*

Games of Infinite Excitement!

オリンピックは無限の興奮！

＊出典：東京2020公式サイト（英語版）https://tokyo2020.org/en/games/venue/
（日本語版）https://tokyo2020.org/jp/games/venue/

インフラ改善に巨大な投資が行われ、
特に旧式だった上下水道は近代化された。

It says that the games then saw huge investment in infrastructure, especially to modernize the old-fashioned water and sewage systems.

Oh, and there's a page here talking about something we already discussed a bit: how the 1964 games changed Tokyo and the image of Japan in the world.

こっちのページには、昨日少し話したことが書いてある。1964年大会がいかに東京と日本のイメージを変えたかという話だ。

Before this, only 25% of houses had flush toilets!

それまでは、水洗トイレのある家は25％しかなかったんだ。

Around 10,000 new buildings were constructed, together with various 5-star hotels, two new subway lines and a monorail from Haneda Airport to the center of Tokyo. It was a key point in opening up Japan to Western and other Asian visitors and changing the bad image of Japan that lingered after WWII to something more positive. The Japanese hope the 2020 games can show the world an up-to-date and improved Tokyo.

10,000ほどの新しいビルが建てられた。いくつもの５つ星ホテルや地下鉄の新路線２つ、そして羽田空港と都心部を結ぶモノレールも。1964年五輪は日本を西洋やアジアに向けて開き、第二次世界大戦後に残っていた悪いイメージを変えるためのキーポイントとなったんだ。2020年五輪では、世界に最新の日本を見せることを日本人は期待してる。

オリンピックの後にはパラリンピックが開催される。パラリンピック聖火リレーが行われるほか、日本各地そしてパラリンピックの生誕地、イギリスのストーク・マンデビルでもお祭りが開催される。

その昔、イギリスのストーク・マンデビル病院にルードウィッヒ・グットマンという神経科医がいて、第二次大戦で脊髄を負傷した兵士たちのリハビリに、スポーツを取り入れていた。

After the Olympic games, the Paralympics will take place, starting with the Paralympic Torch Relay. Various festivals will take place across Japan and also in the birthplace of the Paralympics—the town of Stoke Mandeville in the United Kingdom.

A neurologist called Dr. Ludwig Guttman worked at Stoke Mandeville Hospital in the UK. He used sporting activities as part of the recovery process for soldiers who had spinal injuries from World War II.

大戦後の1948年に行われたロンドン五輪に合わせ、グットマン医師は車椅子の患者たちのためにアーチェリー大会「ストーク・マンデビル競技会」を開いた。

After the war, to tie in with the London 1948 Games, he organized an archery competition for patients in wheelchairs which he named the Stoke Mandeville Games.

Then in 1960, the first Paralympic Games took place in Rome after the Olympic Games were held there. 400 athletes from 23 countries took part in it.

1960年には、ローマ五輪の後に初のパラリンピック大会が開催され、23ヵ国から400人のアスリートが参加した。

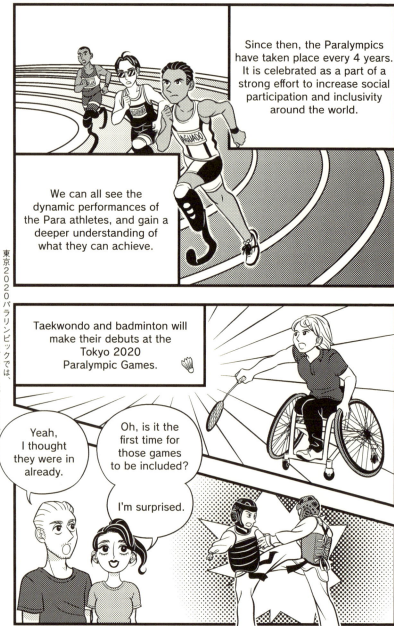

世界が環境に与える影響について意識を高める中、東京五輪は経済的利益と持続可能性の均衡を取ることを目標に開催される。

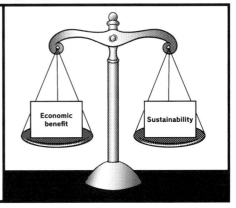

In line with a world increasingly focused on environmental impact, the Tokyo Olympics is being held with the aim of balancing economic benefit with socially sustainable methods.

たとえばメダルには、携帯電話やパソコンなどから抽出した金属が再利用される。川西純市氏によるもので、裏面にはギリシャの勝利の女神ニケがデザインされている。

For example, the metal in phones, PCs, etc has been recycled to make the medals! The designer, Junichi Kawanishi, made a unique design for these 2020 Games, with Nike, the Greek goddess of victor, on the back.

また選手村ビレッジプラザ建築のために各地から無償で提供された木材は、大会終了後には全国の公共施設で活用される。

The lumber used to make the Village Plaza is being donated free, and after the games will be given away for various public facilities to use throughout Japan.

レスリングも強い。
これまで69のメダルだ。

一番有力なのは柔道だよ。
これまで84のメダルを取ってる。

日本はどの競技で期待されてるの？

But also wrestling—69 medals so far.

Well, the obvious one is judo. 84 medals so far.

In which games is Japan expected to do well?

体操は98個のメダル。

Gymnastics—98 medals so far.

And swimming—80 medals so far.

水泳は80だ。

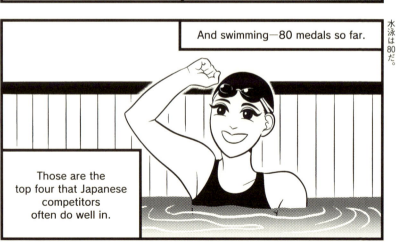

Those are the top four that Japanese competitors often do well in.

この４つが、日本が
よく活躍する競技なんだ。

世界中のあちこちから集まる
大勢の選手の受け入れは
大変でしょう。

How about the preparations for the athletes?

選手受け入れの準備はどうなってるの？

It must be really difficult to prepare for so many from so many different countries.

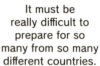

この本によれば、日本の組織委員会は各国の競技団体と何度も協議を行い、ロジスティクスやアスリートへのサービス、施設の出来上がり具合などについて意見を聞いたらしい。

Yes, the book says that extensive meetings were held with various international sports federations, and the Japanese organizing committee for the 2020 Olympics listened to their concerns about event logistics, athlete services, and venue preparedness.

Concerns were raised about the lack of appropriate food, shade and water for athletes at the venues, which the committee made a strong effort to improve.

各競技会場に選手のための適当な食事や日よけ、
そして水がないことが心配されたため、
組織委員会は状況の改善に努力を重ねた。

086

Basic Info about Japan and Tokyo

Currency: Yen
Time zone: GMT+9
Telephone code: +81 for Japan, 3 for Tokyo
Emergency numbers: 110—police, 119—fire/ambulance

日本および東京に関する基本情報
通貨：円
時間帯：GMT＋9時間
電話番号：日本(81)、東京(03)
緊急電話番号：警察 110、消防・救急 119

こんなのが
あるよ。

Yes, here's some:

Hey, how about the basic info everyone needs to know?

みんなに役立つ基本情報は？

東京2020大会の料理・飲み物

Food and Beverage Services at the Tokyo 2020 Games

The Tokyo 2020 Games will offer food
that meets the various needs of all—
competitors, media, and spectators.
The Athletes' Village will have dining facilities serving
Japanese food but also tasty cuisine from around the world.
And, of course, there are plenty of
wonderful restaurants in Tokyo itself!

選手、メディア、観客のさまざまなニーズに合った食べ物が東京2020大会では
提供される予定だ。選手村では日本食の他、世界各国の料理が用意される。
そしてもちろん、都内にはたくさんの素晴らしいレストランがある。

フランスの友達が、チケットが余っていないか知りたがってるのよ。

Because my friend in France said she wondered if there are any tickets left.

なんで？もうチケットは持ってるじゃない。

Why do you want to know that? We've got tickets already.

観戦チケットの買い方は書いてある？

Oh, does it say there how to get tickets?

No, it's too late now. All the tickets have been sold.

もう遅いよ。全部売り切れてる。

WEB SEARCH

Tokyo Okympics 2020 tickets resellers

ALL   NEWS   VIDEOS   IMAGES   SHOPPING

About 1,720,000 results

Authorised Ticket Reseller (T

Our tickets are almost all D tickets, right?

僕たちのチケットはほとんどがD席だよね？

Yes, we're not made of money!

そう。唸るほどお金があるわけじゃないからね。

Prices are dependent on how near the seat is to the main action. "A" tickets are nearest, and "D" tickets furthest away. For example, for the basketball in Saitama Super Arena, the "A" tickets for the first round games are 24,500 yen and the "D" tickets are 5,800 yen.

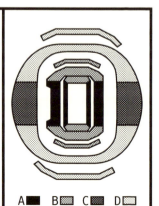

A■　B▦　C▦　D▦

チケットの料金は、座席と競技場との距離によって変わるんだ。A席が一番近く、D席がもっとも遠い。さいたまスーパーアリーナで行われるバスケットボールの試合では、予選のA席は24,500円、D席は5,800円だよ。

088

2020東京大会で予定されていたマラソンコースがこちら。スタートとゴールは新国立競技場で、選手と観客が東京の新旧様々なランドマークを楽しめるようになっていた。しかし酷暑が懸念されるため、マラソン開催地は北海道札幌市に変更された。札幌は東京から1,100キロ北にあるため、東京よりずっと涼しいと考えられている。

This was the planned marathon course set for the 2020 Tokyo Olympics. It would have started and ended at the New National Stadium and taken the runners and fans on a pleasant tour of various landmarks, both modern and traditional. Due to concerns on the extreme summer heat in Tokyo, however, the course was moved to Sapporo City, Hokkaido, which is more than 1,100 km north of Tokyo and considered to be much cooler.

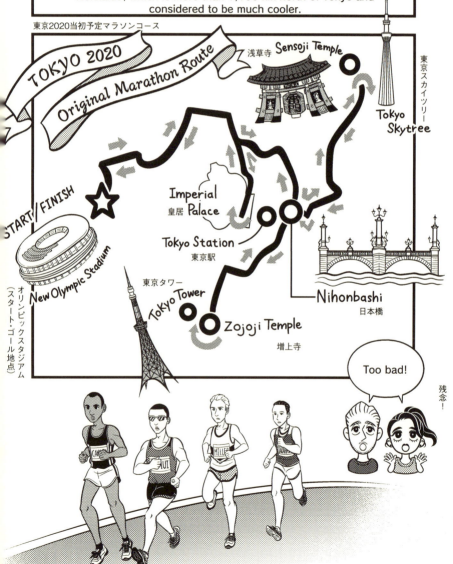

19世紀終わりにフランスの教育者であったピエール・ド・クーベルタンは、
1894年にオリンピック復興を提案したため、「近代オリンピックの父」とされている。

The late-19th century French educator Pierre de Coubertin is widely considered as the father of the modern Olympic Games, having first suggested in 1894 that the ancient games be revived.

彼の尽力により、初の近代オリンピック、1896年夏季五輪は古代オリンピックの生誕地、ギリシャのアテネで開催された。

He pushed hard for this and the first modern Olympic Games, the 1896 Summer Olympics, were held in, appropriately, Athens, Greece.

イギリスのパブリックスクールで競技会を視察したことは彼の考え方に影響を与えた。実際には彼が初めに言ったわけではないようだが「オリンピックは勝つことではなく参加することに意義がある」という言葉で彼は有名になった。

Visiting the sports games of public schools in Britain influenced his views.

Though he was probably not the first to use it, this famous saying is attributed to him:
"The most important thing in the Olympic Games is not winning but taking part."

Organized sport can create character and social strength.

It helps balance the mind and body, and reduces wasteful activities.

競技スポーツは倫理的・社会的な力を育む。
心身のバランスを保つのに役立つだけでなく、
無駄な行動をすることを防ぐ。

〈応援で使える便利フレーズ〜「がんばれ！」を英語で言ってみよう〉

　喜んだり悲しんだり、エキサイトして怒ったり……自分でやるときも観戦するときも、スポーツはさまざまな感情を呼び起こします。ここでは、応援するときに使える英語のフレーズを見てみましょう。まずは、「がんばれ」の言い方です。英語には同じように対応する言葉がないので、状況に合わせて言葉を使い分けましょう。以下では試合前と試合中に分けていますが、どちらでも使える場合がほとんどです。

　各フレーズにはカタカナでの読み方を付け、強く発音する箇所は太字で示しました。どれも気持ちをこめて言うのがポイントです！

＊試合前の「がんばれ」＊

□ Go for it!　ゴウ　フォー　イッ(ト)
　がんばって！

□ Go get 'em!　ゴウ　**ゲ**ッテム
　がんばれ！

□ We're all rooting for you!　ウィア　オール　**ルー**ティング　フォー　ユー
　みんな応援してるよ！

□ Do your best!　ドゥ　ユア　ベス(ト)
　がんばってベストを尽くして！

□ Give it all you got!　**ギ**ヴィッ(ト)　オール　ユー　**ガッ**(ト)
　全力を尽くしてがんばれ！

□ Knock 'em dead!　ナッケム　デッ(ド)
　やっつけちゃえ！

＊試合中の「がんばれ」＊

□ Go for it!　ゴウ　フォー　イッ(ト)
　やれー！／がんばれー！

□ Come on!　カモン
　がんばって！

□ You can do it!　ユー　キャン　**ドゥ**　イッ(ト)
　できるよ！

□ Go, go, go!　ゴウ　ゴウ　ゴウ
　行け行け行けー！

□ Nice try!　**ナ**イス　トゥライ
　よくがんばった！

〈応援で使える便利フレーズ〜ハラハラドキドキを表わしてみる〉

応援している選手やチームがピンチのとき、また、そのピンチを脱したときなどに使えるフレーズです。

＊ピンチのとき＊

☐ Ohh, I can't watch this.　オーゥ　アイ　**キャン**（ト）　ウォッチ　ディス
あー、見てられない。

☐ I can't believe this is happening.
アイ　**キャン**（ト）　ビリーヴ　ディス　イズ　**ハ**プニング
こんなことが起きるなんて信じられない。

☐ No way!　ノウ　**ウェ**イ
うそでしょ！

☐ Oh darn!　オウ　**ダ**ーン
なんてことだ！

☐ Nooo!　ノ——ゥ
ダメ———！

＊ピンチを脱したとき＊

☐ He missed! I knew it!　ヒー　**ミ**ス（ド）　アイ　**ニュ**ー　イッ（ト）
ゴールを外した！　外れると思ってたよ！

☐ Way to go!　**ウェ**イ　トゥ　ゴウ
よくやった！

☐ Wow, he's so strong!　ワウ　ヒーズ　ソウ　**ストゥ**ロング
彼、すごく強いね！

☐ Great play!　グ**レイ**（ト）　プレイ
ナイスプレー！

☐ Yes! She's the best!　**イェ**ス　シーズ　ザ　**ベ**ス（ト）
よくやった！　彼女、最高だね！

☐ Nice catch!　**ナ**イス　**キャ**ッチ
よく取った！

☐ Nice run!　**ナ**イス　ラン
いい走り！

〈応援で使える便利フレーズ〜うれしい気持ち、悲しい気持ちを表現する〉

試合は真剣勝負、勝つ人がいれば負ける人もいますね。それぞれのシチュエーションに合ったフレーズを見てみましょう。

＊勝ったとき＊

□ We won!　ウィー　ワン
勝った！

□ Awesome!　オーサム
最高！

□ Fantastic!　ファンタスティック
素晴らしい！

□ They're the best team ever!　ゼイア　ザ　ベスト　ティーム　エヴァー
史上最高のチームだ！

□ He's the best player on earth!
ヒーズ　ザ　ベスト　プレイヤー　オン　アース
彼は世界中で最高の選手だ！

□ Yeees!　イエース
やったー！

＊負けたとき＊

□ We lost.　ウィー　ロス（ト）
負けた。

□ Too bad.　トゥー　バッ（ド）
残念だったね。

□ I can't believe it.　アイ　キャン（ト）　ビリーヴィッ（ト）
信じられない。

□ They were too strong.　ゼイ　ワー　トゥー　ストゥロング
相手が強すぎたね。

□ Let's look forward to the next Olympics.
レッツ　ルック　フォワー（ド）　トゥ　ザ　ネクスト　オリンピックス
次のオリンピックを楽しみにしよう。

〈応援で使える便利フレーズ〜お互いの健闘を称える〉

　試合が終わったら、互いに健闘を称えあいましょう。他国を応援している相手と握手するのもいいですね。

☐ Japan played well today. Good game.
　　ジャパン　プレイ(ド)　**ウェ**ル　トゥデイ　**グッ**ゲイム
　　日本は今日よく戦った。いい試合だったね。
　　—Thanks. Australia also!　**サン**クス　オースト**レイ**リア　**オー**ルソウ
　　ありがとう。オーストラリアもね。

☐ I enjoyed the game very much. Thank you.
　　アイ　エン**ジョイ**ド　ザ　**ゲイ**ム　ヴェ**リィ**　**マッ**チ　**サン**キュー
　　とても面白い試合だったよ。ありがとう。

☐ Great game!　グ**レイ**(ト)　**ゲイ**ム
　　素晴らしい試合だった！

☐ It was a good match.　イッ(ト)　ワズ　ア　**グッ**(ド)　**マッ**チ
　　いい試合だった。

☐ Your country's performance was wonderful.
　　ユア　**カン**トリーズ　パ**フォー**マンス　ワズ　**ワン**ダフル
　　あなたの国の演技は素晴らしかった。

☐ I've become a fan of Kenya's team.
　　アイヴ　ビカム　ア　**ファン**　オヴ　**ケ**ニアズ　ティーム
　　ケニアチームのファンになったよ。

☐ She's a wonderful player. I hope she wins the gold medal.
　　シーズ　ア　**ワン**ダフル　プ**レイ**ヤー　アイ　**ホウ**プ　シー　**ウィ**ンズ　ザ　**ゴウ**ルド
　　メダル
　　彼女は素晴らしい選手だね。金メダルが取れますように。

☐ Congratulations on the gold medal!
　　コング**ラ**チュレイシャンズ　オン　ザ　**ゴウ**ルド　**メ**ダル
　　金メダルおめでとう！

☐ See you again in four years.
　　ス**ィー**　ユー　ア**ゲ**ン　イン　**フォー**　イヤーズ
　　4年後にまた会おう。

会話のコツ③

自分の意見を言うときのフレーズを中心に取り上げます。マンガの場面も参考にしてくださいね。

☐ **I don't think I could handle that.** 僕には無理かも。(p.74)
「それはもう十分だ、それは対応できない」という気持ちを表わすときに使う表現です。
例)You're going to another bar? I don't think I could handle that. もう一軒バーに寄るって？ 僕には無理かな。
They won't extend the deadline? Well, I don't think we could handle that. 締切りを延ばしてくれないって？ それ、私たちには対応できないと思う。

☐ **I'm surprised that** any of the 1964 venues are still there.
前回の施設がまだあるなんて、驚いたわ。(p.75)
驚いたとき、thatでつなげてその理由も述べてみましょう。
例)I'm surprised that we all got tickets for the closing ceremony. 閉会式のチケットが全員手に入って、驚いたよ。
I'm surprised that Japanese people can stand such crowded trains. 日本人はあんなに混んでいる電車に耐えられるなんて、びっくりだわ。

☐ **That sounds really good.** よさそうなアイディアね。(p.82)
よい意見や話を聞いたときは、こう言ってみましょう。文頭のthatは省略できるほか、thisやitなども使えます。
例)You're planning to have a party at the new Brazilian restaurant? Sounds really good. 新しくできたブラジル料理のお店でパーティをするんだって？ よさそうだね。
Lisa will take care of the guests. She's good with people so this sounds really good. お客様の対応はリサがする。彼女は人と接するのがうまいから、よさそうだね。

☐ I'm glad that they **care about** the old-style Japanese culture.
日本の古い文化を大切にするひとがいて嬉しいわ。(p.83)
care about...で「…を大切にする」という意味になり、いろいろな場面で使えます。
例)Henry and his wife care about their parents and look after them well. ヘンリー夫妻は自分たちの両親を大切にし、よく面倒を見ています。
Our company cares about the environment so we take part in various nature conservation projects. わが社は環境を大切にしているので、様々な自然保護活動に参加しています。

098

Part 4:
Epilogue—Opening Ceremony
エピローグ～開会式

The Newest Venue

最新の会場
  Venue capacity: 68,000
  収容人数：68,000

Olympic Stadium (designed by Kengo Kuma)
オリンピックスタジアム（隈研吾設計）

Shinjuku Gyoen National Garden

Samurai Museum

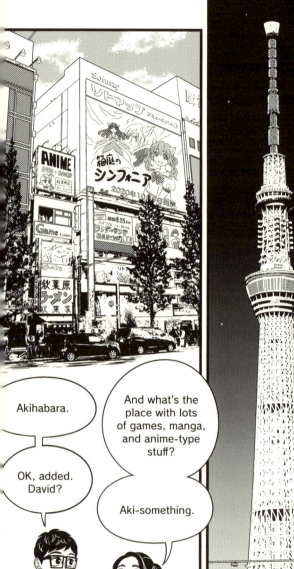

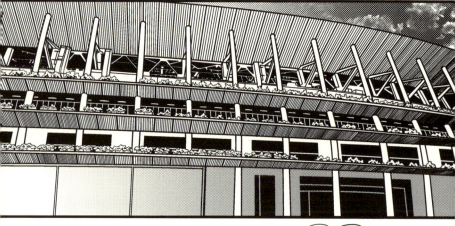

会話のコツ④

提案したり、希望を述べたりするのはよくあること。そんなときは次の言い回しを使ってみましょう。

- [ ] **I heard that** Shinjuku Gyoen National Garden is beautiful.
  新宿御苑がきれいだって聞いたわ。(p.101)
  heard that . . .「…ということを聞いた」を使って、聞き知った内容について話してみましょう。
- 例)I heard that Meghna only eats halal food. メグナはハラル料理しか食べないと聞いたよ。
  We heard that Beppu has wonderful hot springs so we would like to visit there one day. 別府には素晴らしい温泉があると聞いたので、いつか行ってみたいと思います。

- [ ] **I also suggest** Ueno Park and Tokyo Skytree.
  上野公園や東京スカイツリーもおすすめだよ。(p.102)
  何かを提案するときに使えるフレーズです。
- 例)You want to see sumo wrestlers? Then I suggest Ryogoku, where there are many sumo stables. 力士が見たいって？ それなら相撲部屋がたくさんある両国をおすすめするよ。
  If you like food, I suggest visiting *depa-chika*, the basement floor of department stores. 食べ物が好きなら、デパ地下に行くのはおすすめだね。

- [ ] I'd like to **check out** the nightlife in Shibuya and Shinjuku.
  渋谷と新宿のナイトライフを見てみたいな。(p.103)
  check out . . .は「…を見てみる、行ってみる」の意味で、よく口語で使われます。
- 例)Can we check out that shop we just passed by? 今通り過ぎたお店を覗いてみてもいい？
  Let's go check out who's performing at the live house. ライブハウスで誰が演奏するのか見てみよう。

- [ ] What, that's **way** too much! それは高すぎるな。(p.104)
  このwayは強調で使われていて、「あまりに〜」という意味になります。これも口語的な表現です。
- 例)You want to walk to Tokyo Tower? That's way too far. 東京タワーまで歩きたいって？ それは遠すぎるよ。
  His ideas are way ahead of time. 彼の発想は時代のはるか先を行っている。

p.43の渋谷の絵は、以下を参考にしています。
『渋谷の記憶Ⅳ 写真で見る今と昔』p.68
編集・発行　渋谷区教育委員会

KODANSHA BILINGUAL COMICS
バイリンガル・コミックス 英語でガイドする東京+オリンピック

2019年12月10日　第1刷発行

原　作	ショーン・マイケル・ウィルソン
漫　画	Makiko Kodama
翻　訳	深井裕美子
発行者	渡瀬昌彦
発行所	株式会社　講談社 〒112-8001　東京都文京区音羽2-12-21 販売　TEL 03-5395-3606 業務　TEL 03-5395-3615
編　集	株式会社　講談社エディトリアル
代　表	堺 公江 〒112-0013　東京都文京区音羽1-17-18 護国寺SIAビル　TEL 03-5319-2171
装　幀	イオック
印刷所	豊国印刷株式会社
本文製版所	豊国印刷株式会社
製本所	株式会社国宝社

定価はカバーに表示してあります。
落丁本・乱丁本は購入書店名を明記のうえ、小社業務宛にお送りください。送料当社負担にてお取り替えいたします。
なお、この本のお問い合わせは、講談社エディトリアル宛にお願いします。
本書のコピー、スキャン、デジタル化等の無断複製は著作権法上の例外を除き、禁じられています。本書を代行業者等の第三者に依頼してスキャンやデジタル化することはたとえ個人や家庭内の利用でも著作権法違反です。

© Sean Michael Wilson, Makiko Kodama, Yumiko Fukai 2019
Printed in Japan
ISBN978-4-06-518163-8